Preschool Handwriting

Susan Young

illustrations by Janice Bowles

My name is

____

Introduction

This workbook introduces the prep student to the Basic Movements of handwriting.
These movements are the building blocks for writing letters and they support the formation of Beginners Script.

BASIC MOVEMENTS INCLUDE:

Straight line	Anticlockwise	Clockwise	Anticlockwise and clockwise
Downstroke Horizontal Diagonal upstroke and downstroke Crisscross 'z' pattern	Movement 'w' pattern Loop pattern	'm' pattern Loop pattern 'j' pattern	's' pattern

This book is designed to supplement the *Teachers' Preschool Handwriting Program.* Gross motor skills and fine motor skills are also part of the Preschool students' daily routine, and are essential for the development of good handwriting skills.

Gross motor skills help develop coordination and strength. The use of major muscle groups involve activities such as balancing, catching, climbing, hopping, jumping, skipping, kicking, rolling, running, throwing and walking.

Fine motor skills activities can include colouring in, construction toys, counters, craft, cutting, dot-to-dot, dough/plasticine modelling, drawing, finger plays, hammering, jigsaws, keyboarding, painting, painting with ear buds (this is an excellent activity for practising the tripod grip), pasting, sewing, sorting, beads/buttons, threading and weaving. Writing on scrap paper using a variety of instruments should also be encouraged.

Small-group work is preferable to whole-class instruction. Small groups allow the teacher to deal more effectively with the differing handwriting abilities within the class. They also allow the teacher to closely monitor Pencil, Pencil grip, Posture and Placement of workbook.

Handy hint: *Introduce each basic movement by having students trace it with their fingers. They can trace the pattern in the air, on their desks or even on a friend's back!*

PRESCHOOL HANDWRITING WORKBOOK FEATURES

- Instructions and activities are simple and repetitive, allowing the student to concentrate on the writing task.
- The first set of activities encourages left-to-right movement, using a series of tracks and pathways.
- Basic movement patterns are introduced on each double page. Even numbered pages feature the large practice activities. Odd numbered pages have slightly smaller activities with the accompanying fluency pattern.
- Fluency patterns and basic movements are explored in a more formal way in the final section of the book. To maintain natural hand movements pencil lifts have been incorporated into the fluency patterns.

Hint: *Some students may find smaller activities hard to achieve in the early stages of Preschool. Teachers may wish to introduce the even pages first, and then as the year progresses introduce the odd numbered pages. This way the basic movement patterns can be revised, and students will have had time to develop the skills necessary for the smaller activities.*

I hope you and your students enjoy using this book.

Susan Young

Contents

MECHANICS OF HANDWRITING

Posture

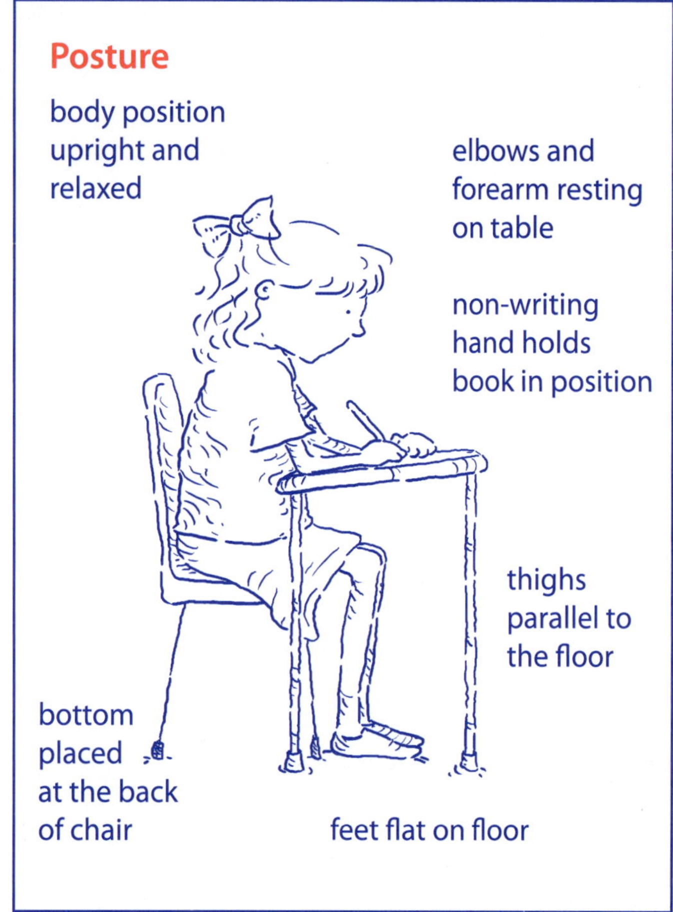

Paper position

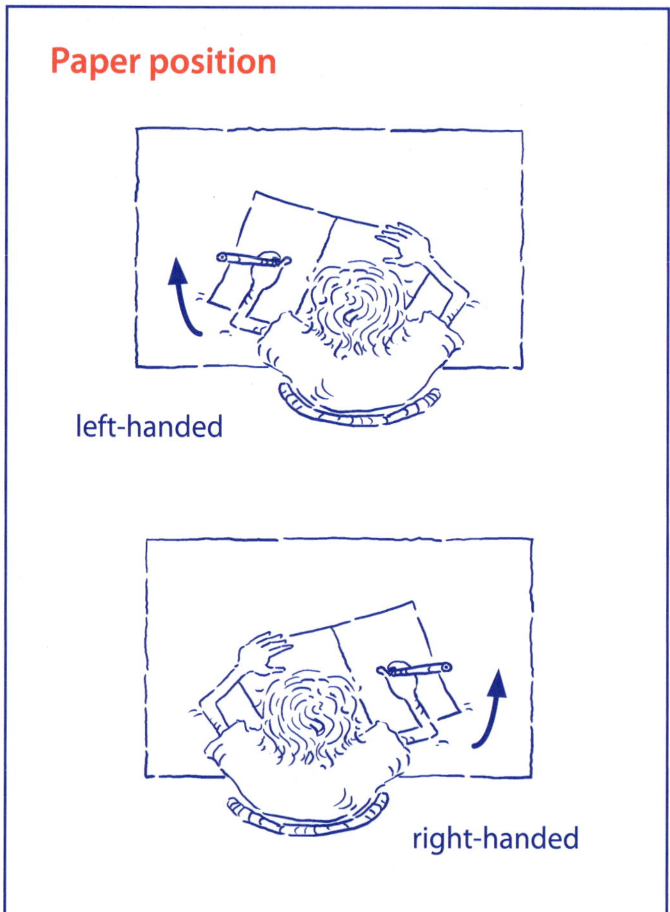

Pencil grip

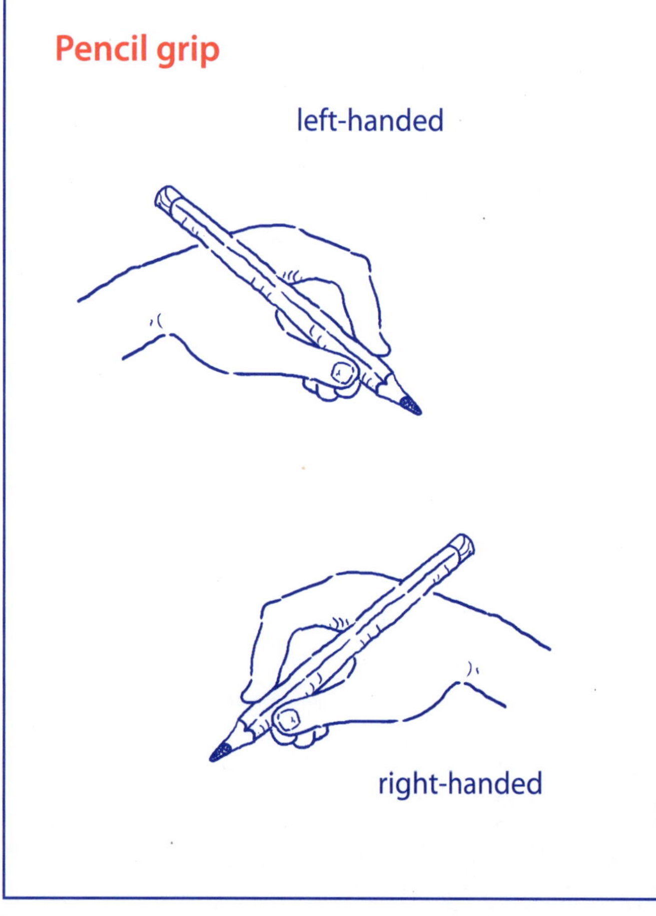

Pencil

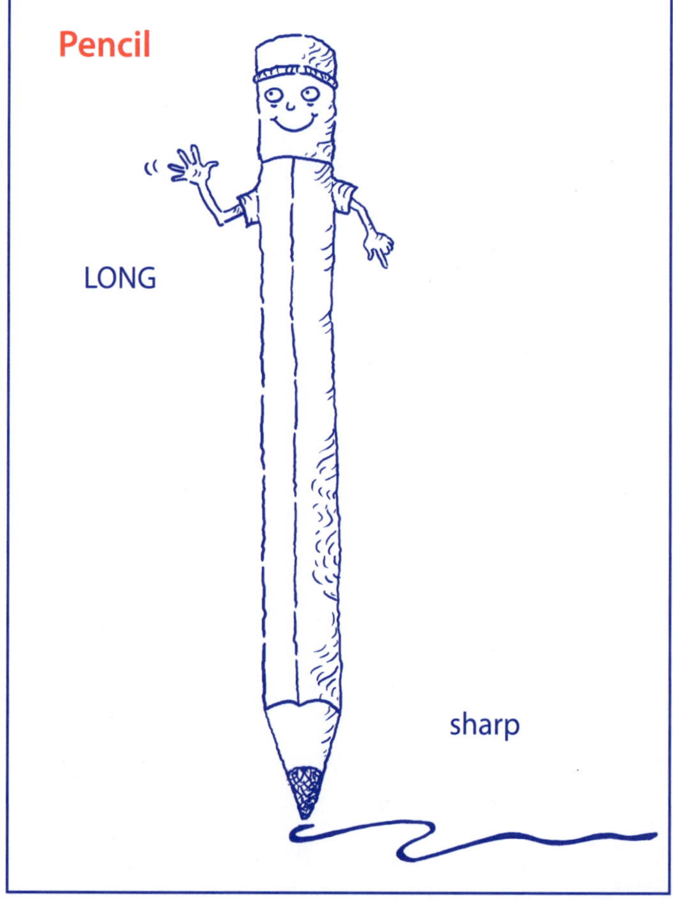

Follow the track. Start at the red dot.

Follow the path. Start at the red dot.

Trace the snail trails. Start at the red dot.

Trace. Start at the red dot.

Trace. Start at the red dot.

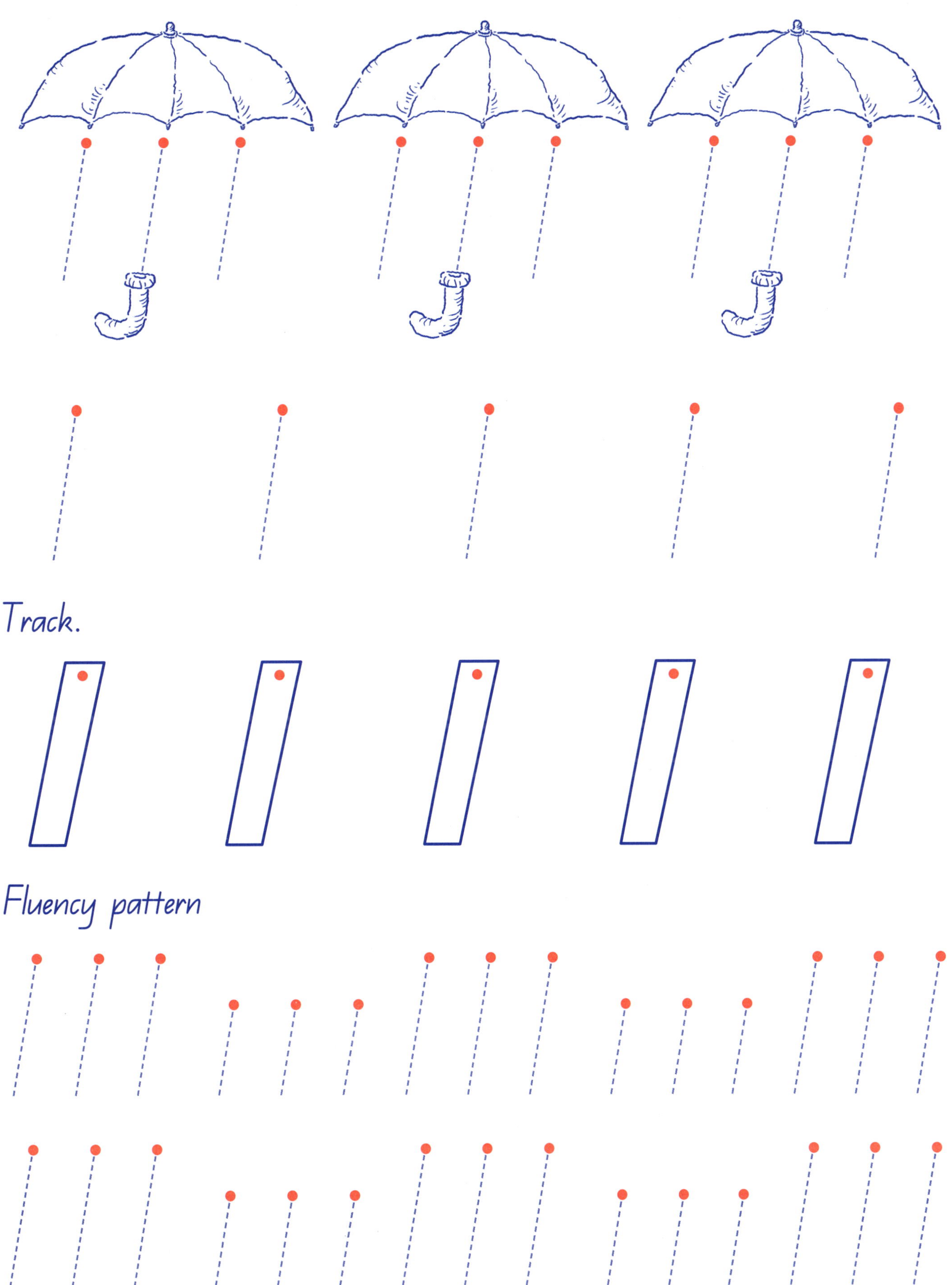

Track.

Fluency pattern

Trace. Start at the red dot.

Trace. Start at the red dot.

Track.

Fluency pattern

Trace. Start at the red dot.

Trace. Start at the red dot.

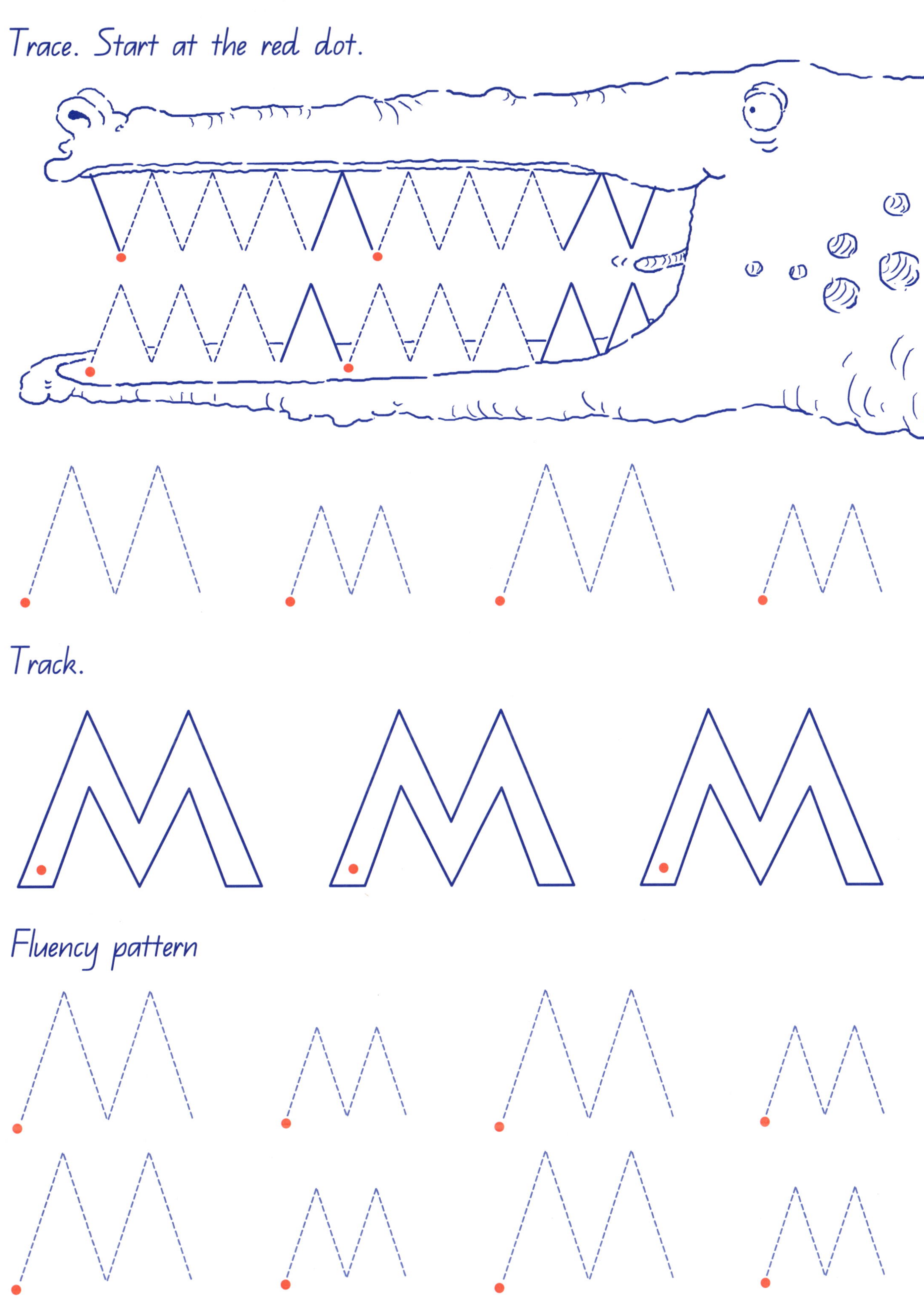

Track.

Fluency pattern

Trace. Start at the red dot.

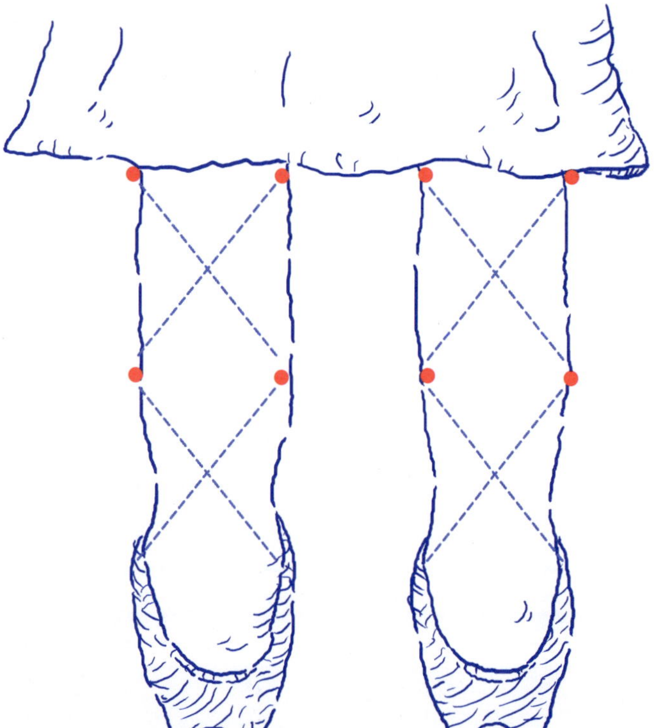

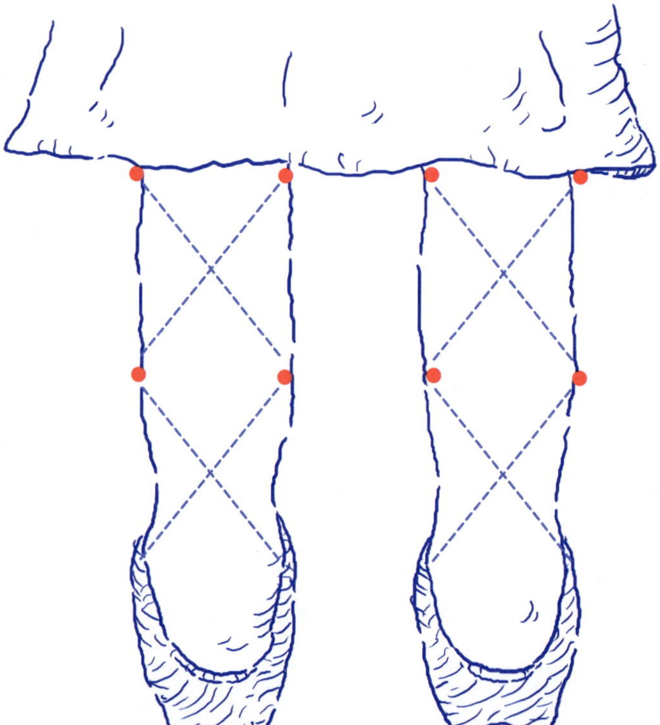

Trace. Start at the red dot.

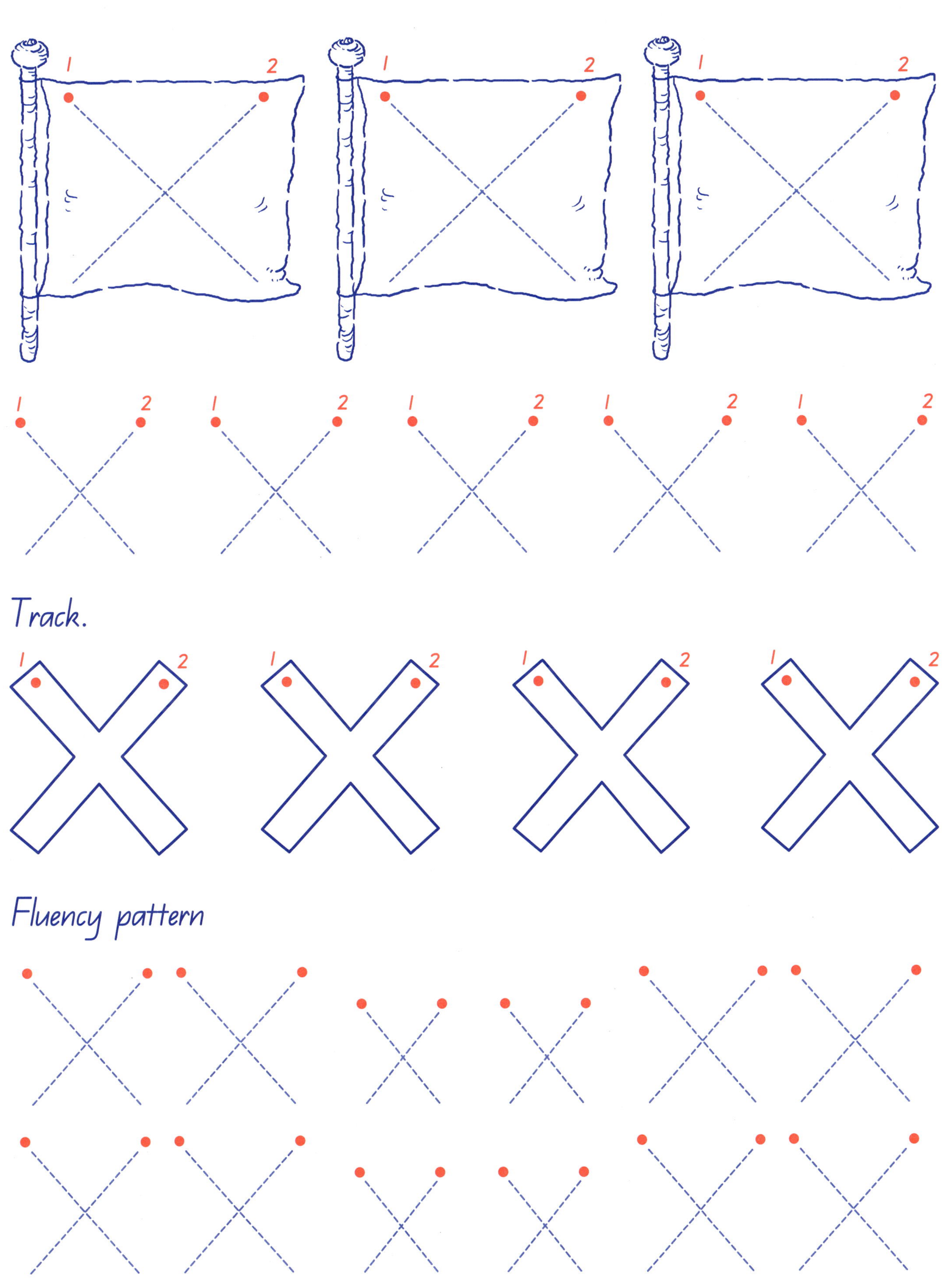

Track. Start at the red dot.

Track. Start at the red dot.

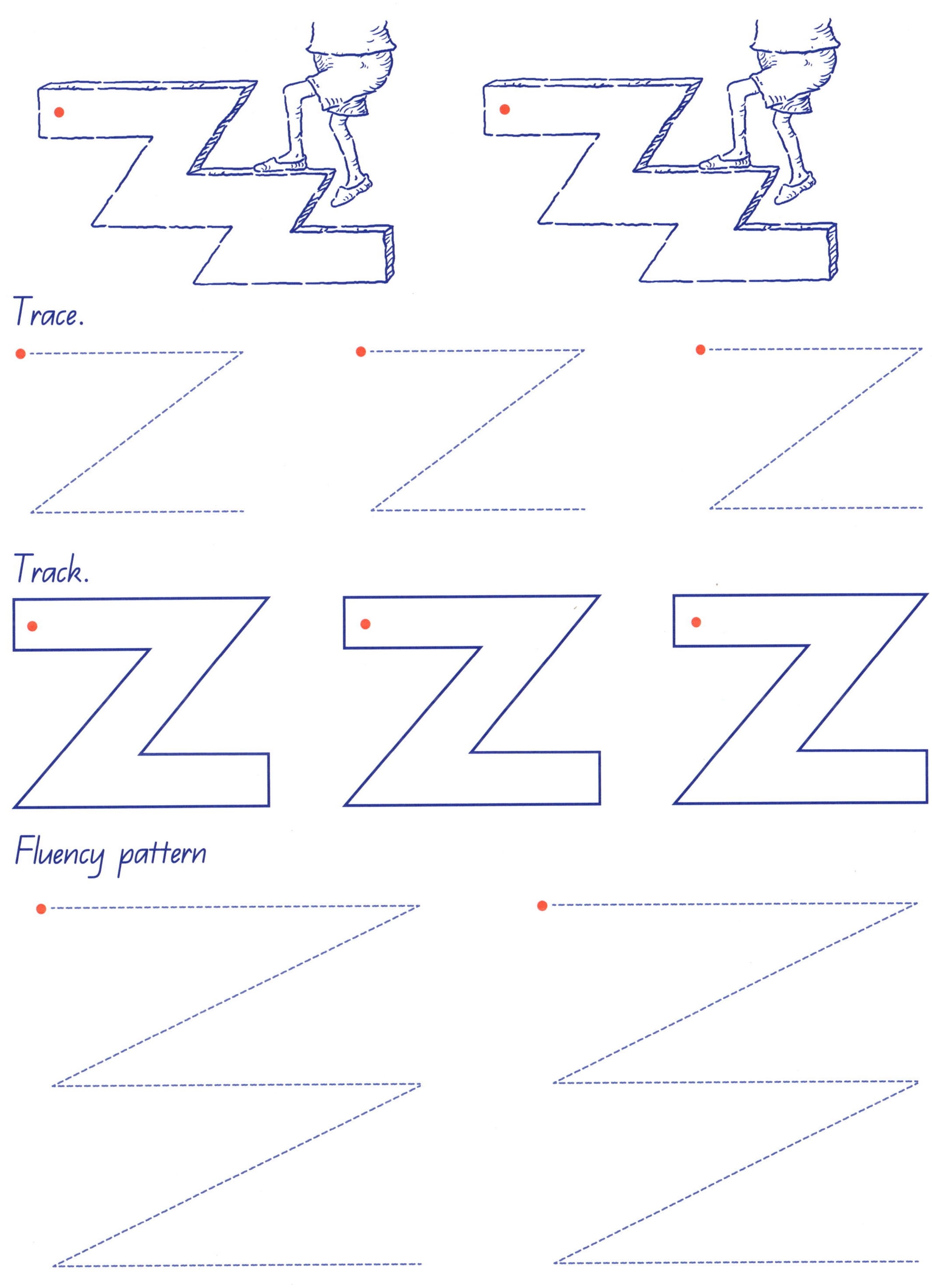

Trace.

Track.

Fluency pattern

Trace.

Track.

Trace. Start at the red dot.

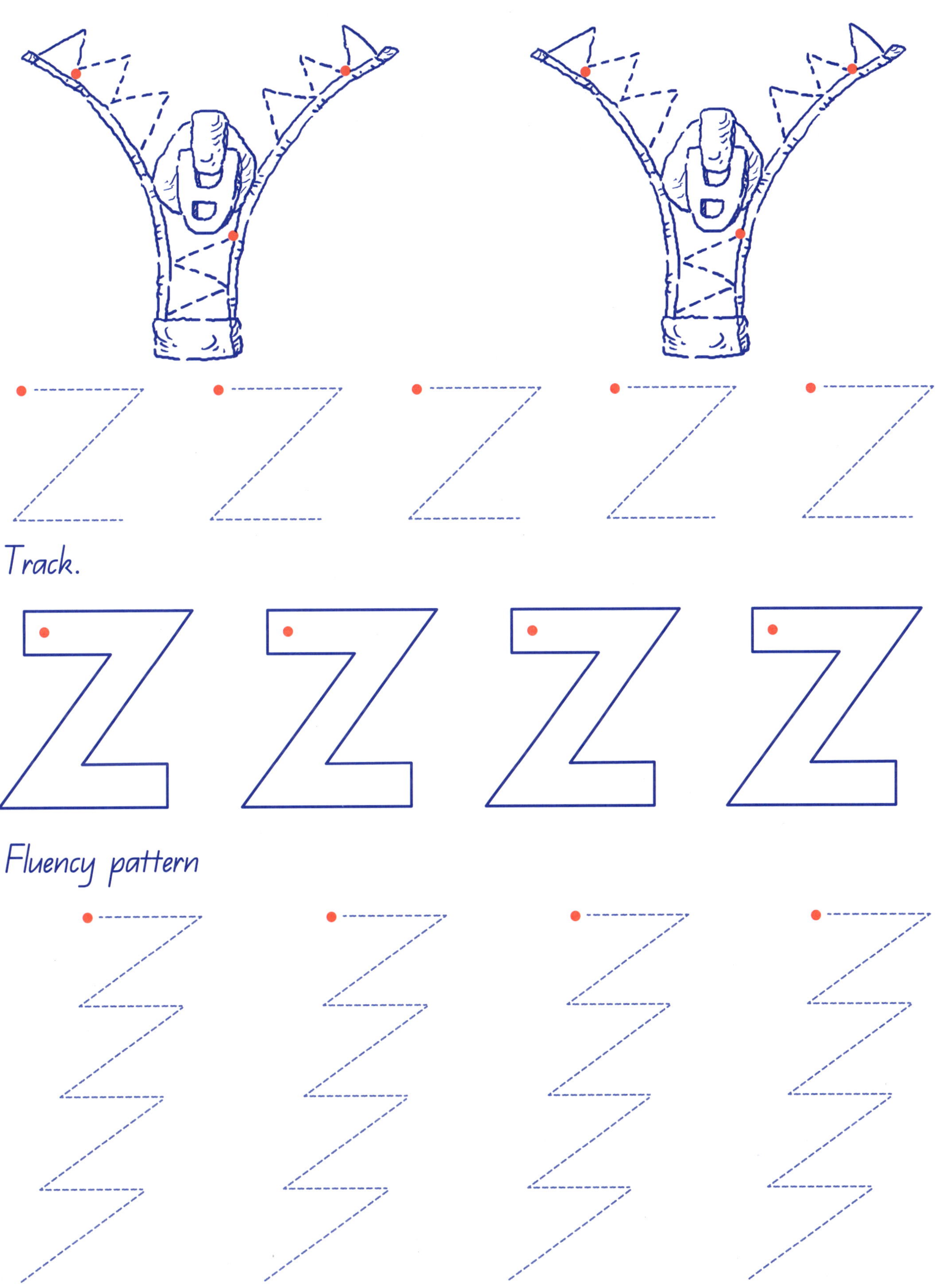

Track.

Fluency pattern

Trace. Start at the red dot.

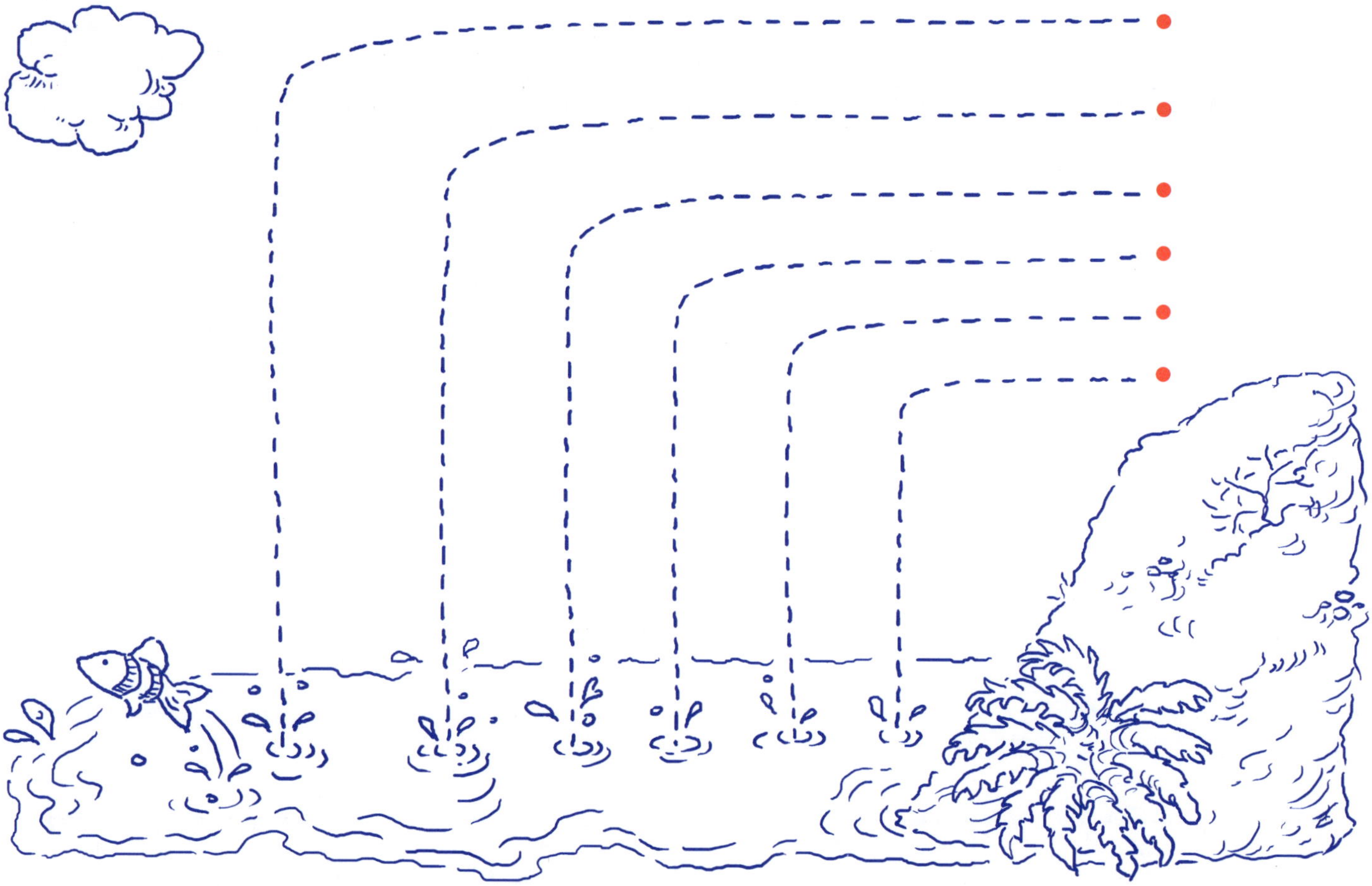

Anticlockwise pattern

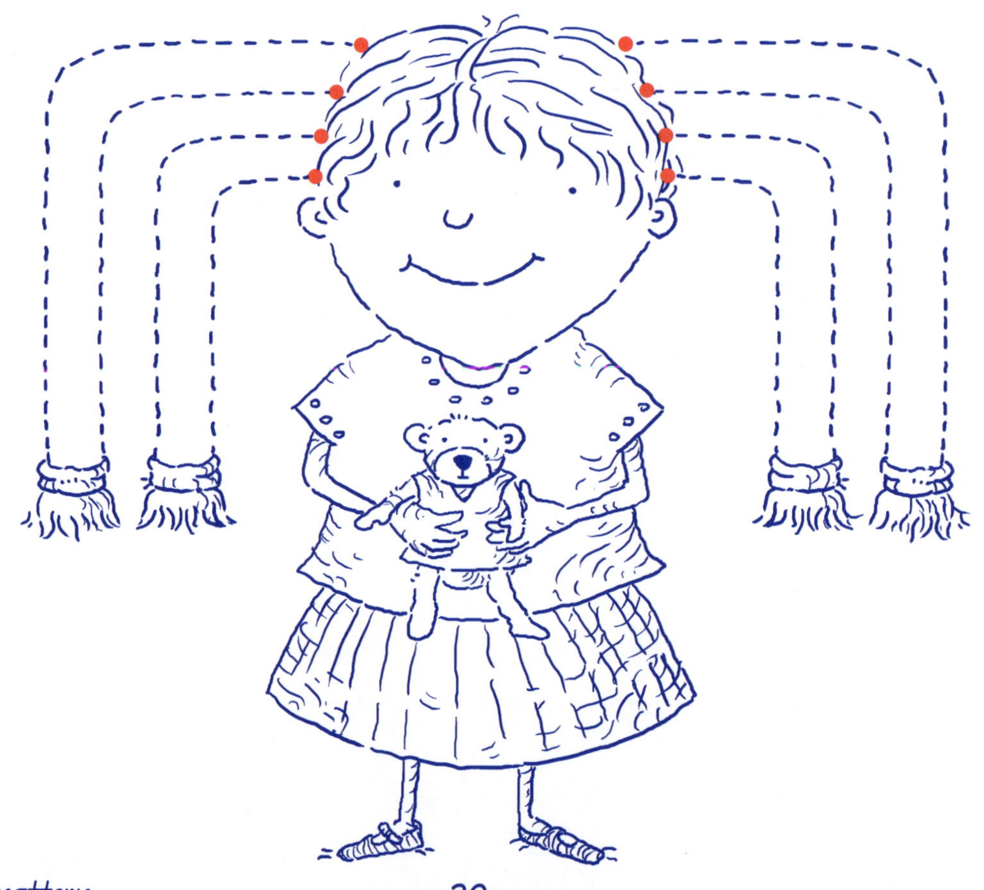

Trace. Start at the red dot.

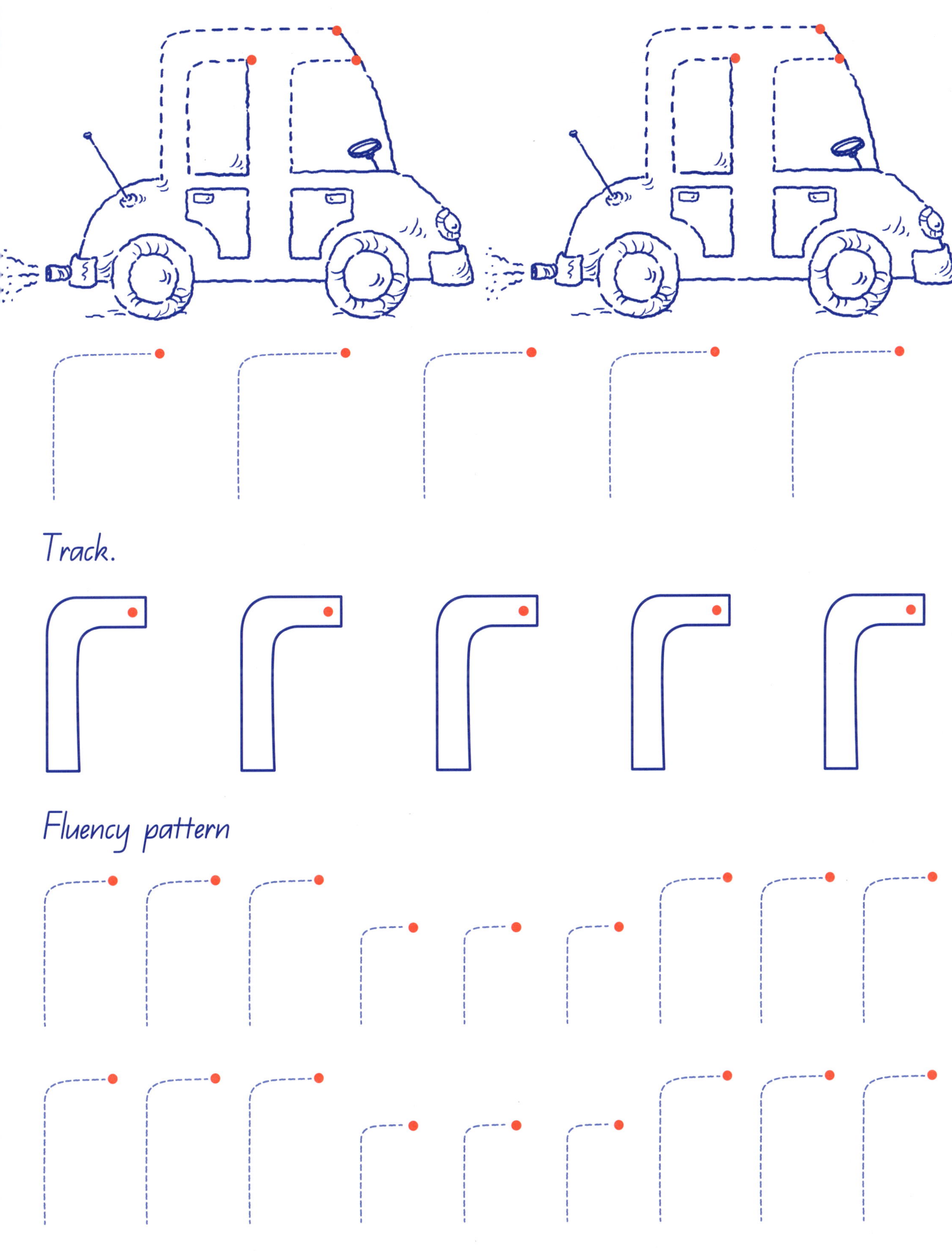

Track.

Fluency pattern

Trace. Start at the red dot.

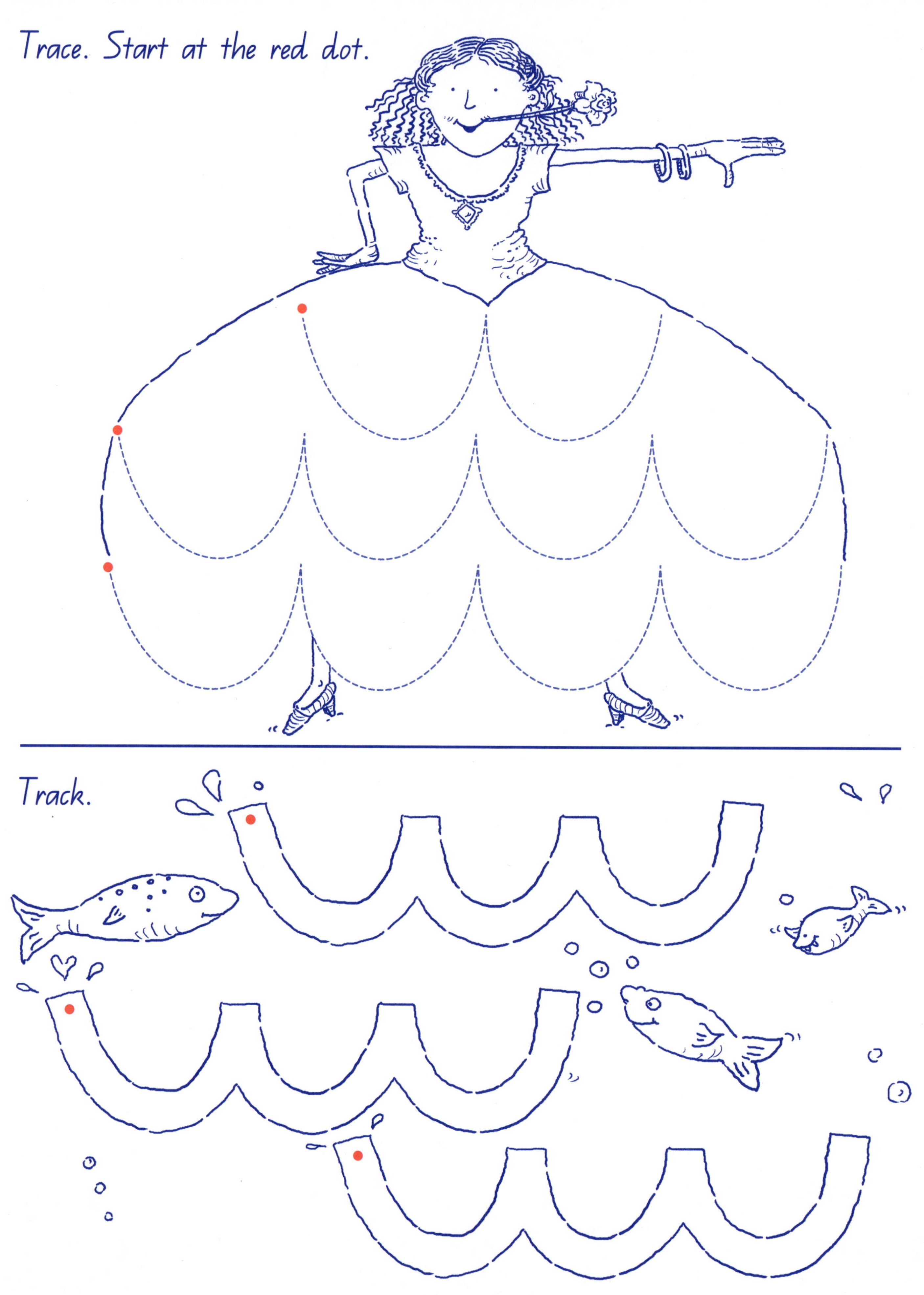

Track.

Trace. Start at the red dot.

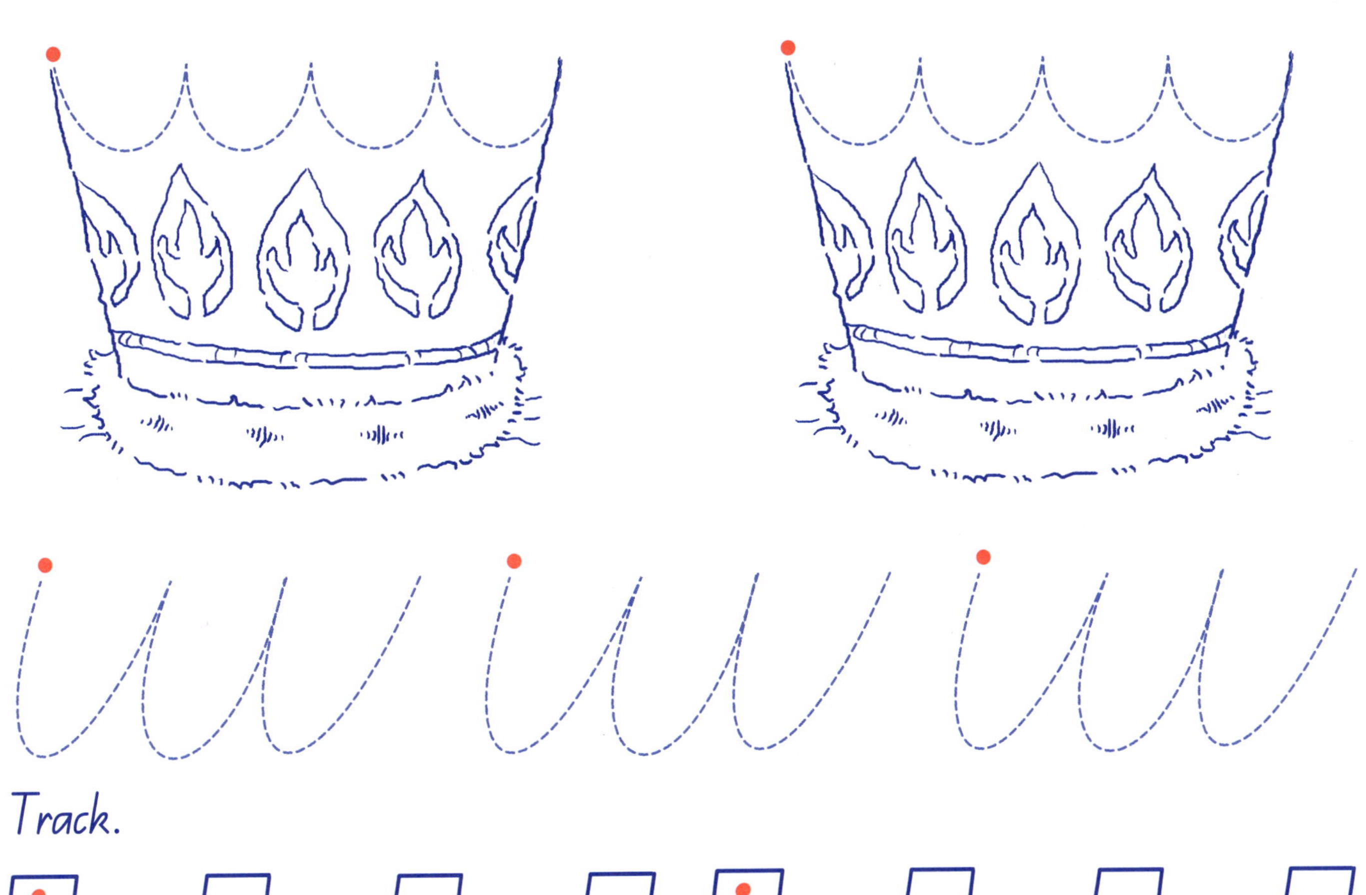

Track.

Fluency pattern

Trace. Start at the red dot.

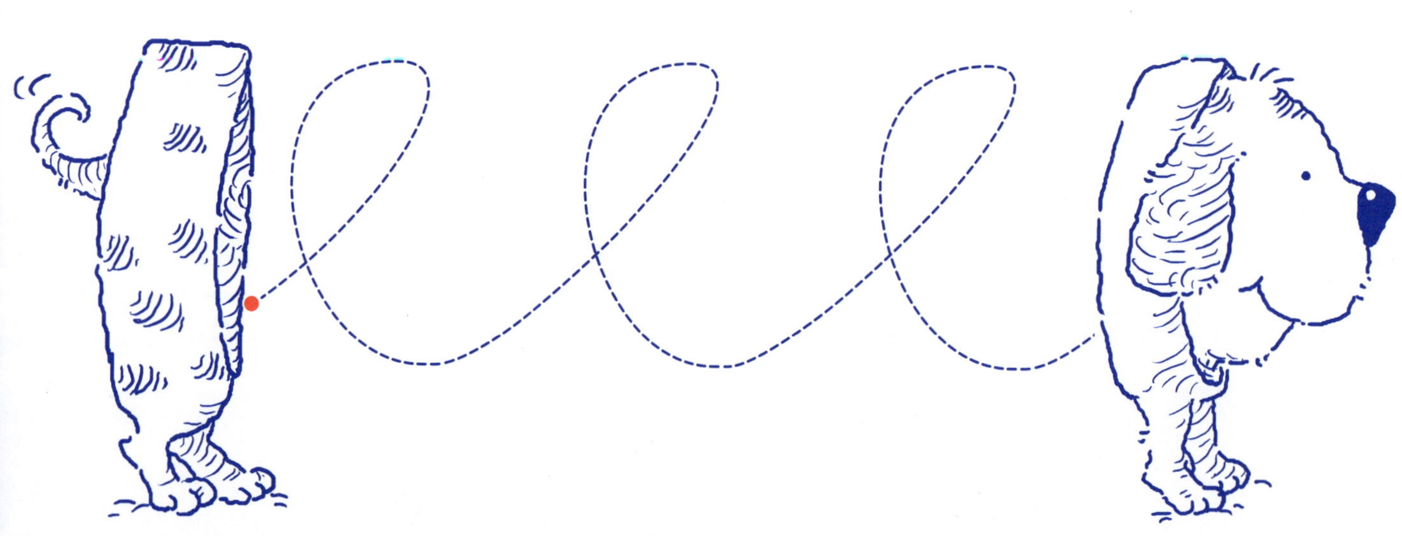

Anticlockwise – loop pattern

Trace. Start at the red dot.

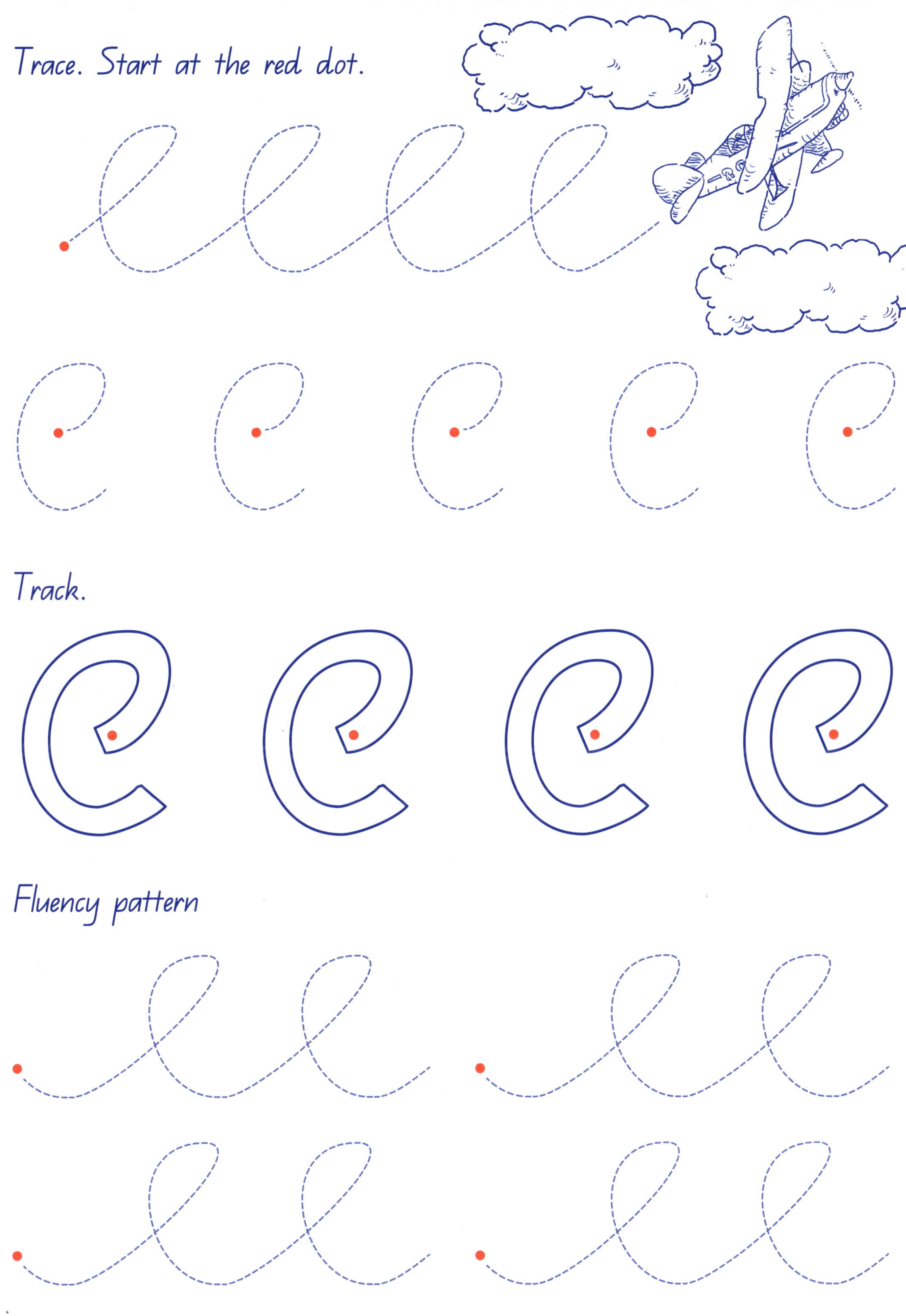

Track.

Fluency pattern

Trace. Start at the red dot.

Track.

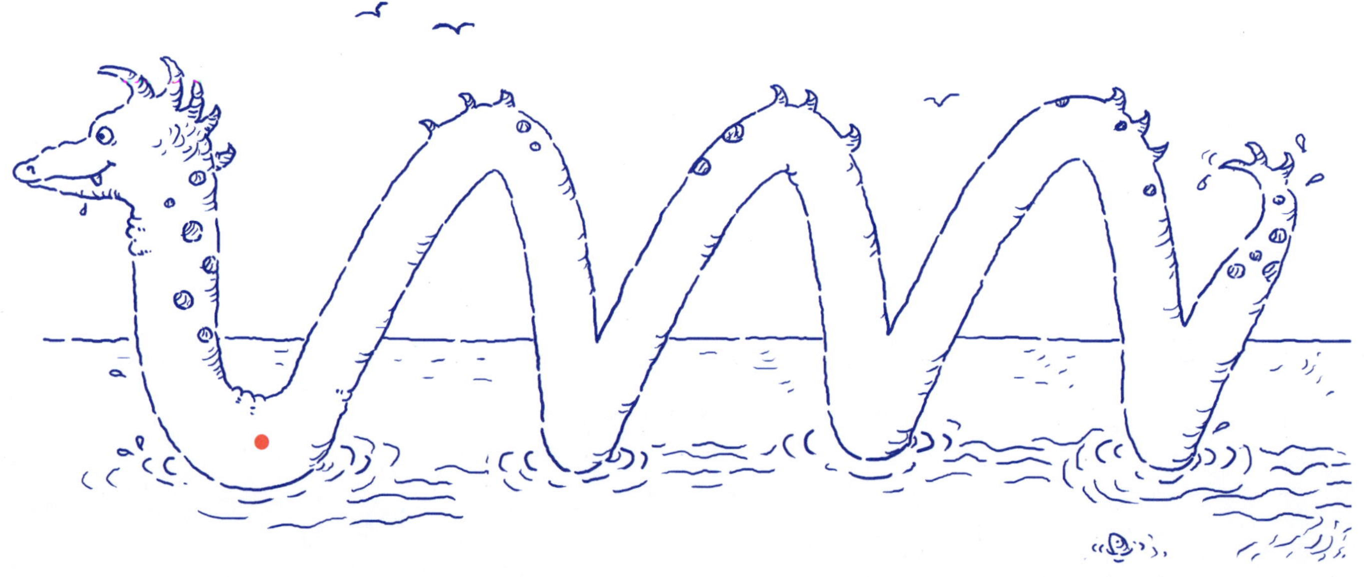

Trace. Start at the red dot.

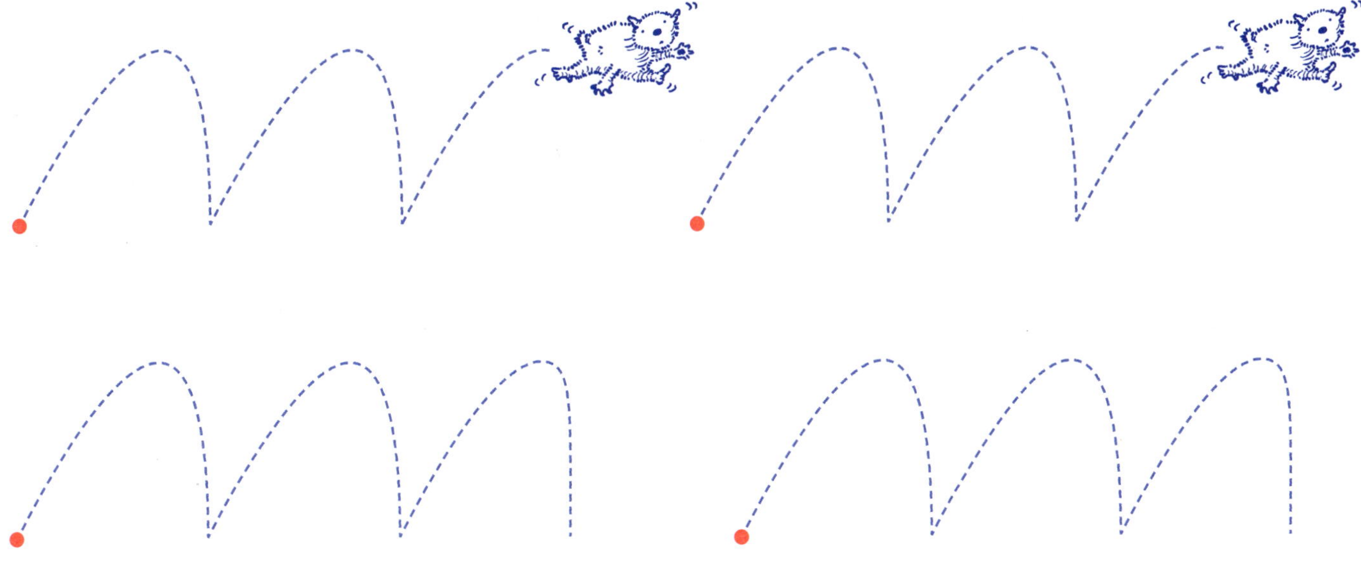

Track.

Fluency pattern

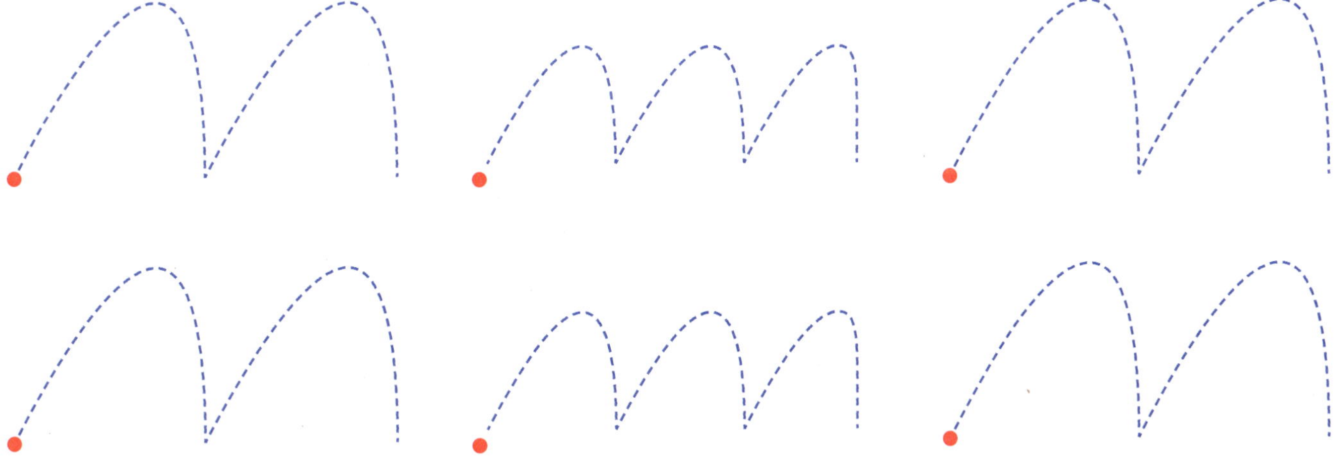

Trace. Start at the red dot.

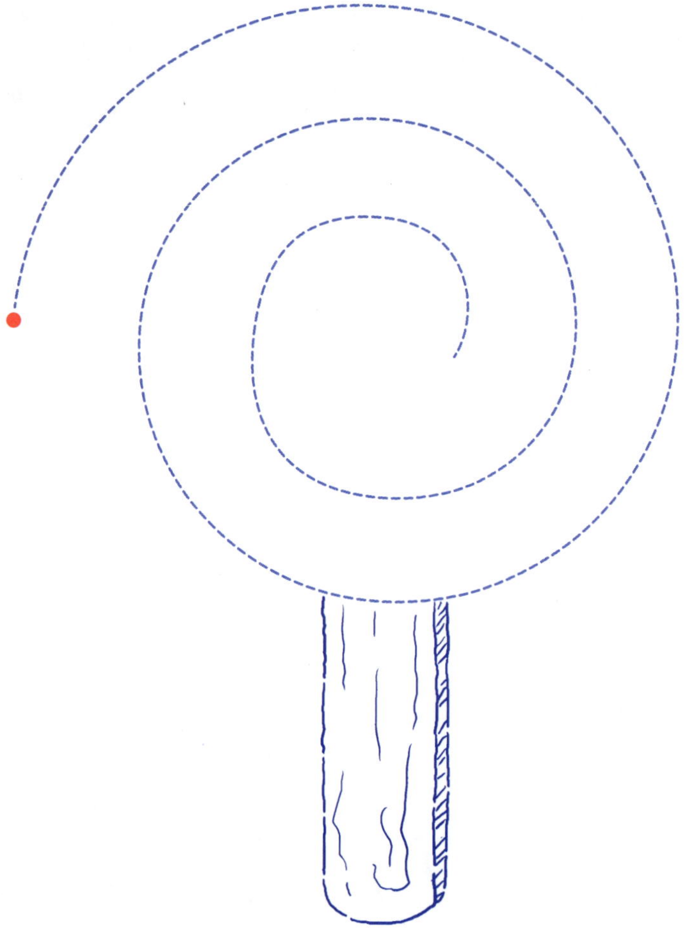

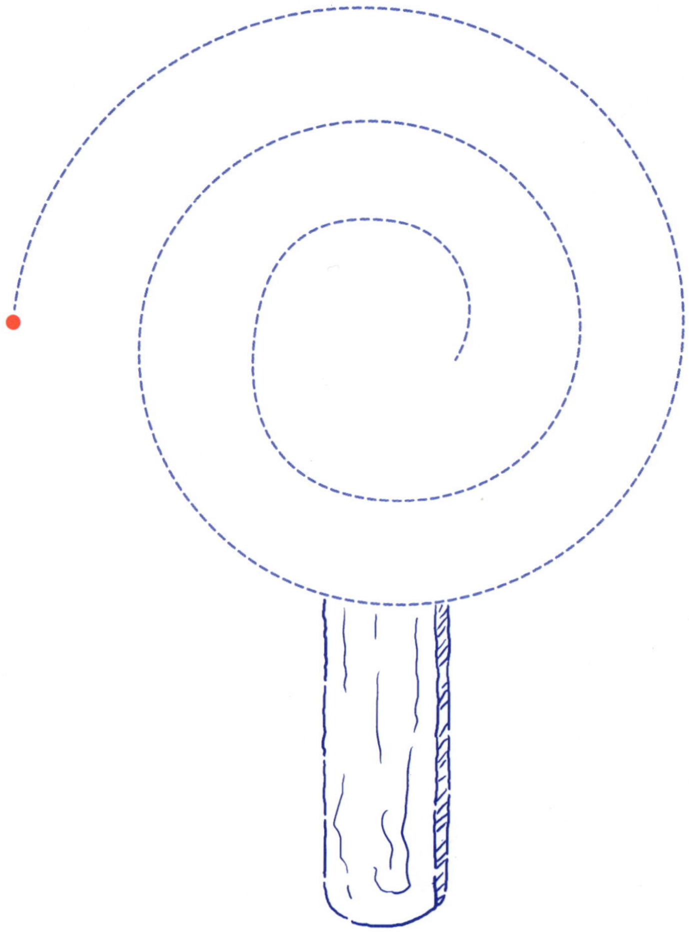

Track.

Trace. Start at the red dot.

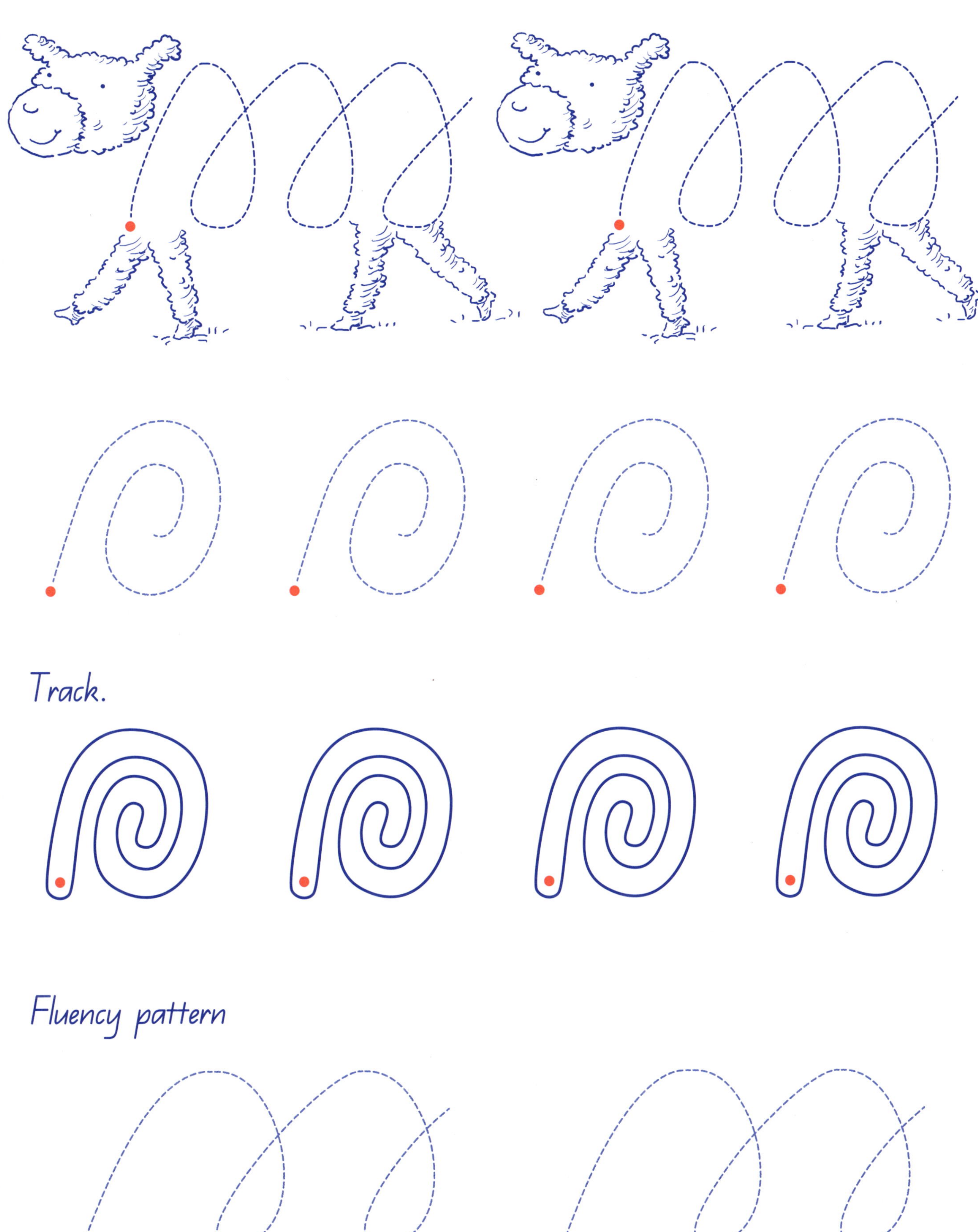

Track.

Fluency pattern

Trace. Start at the red dot.

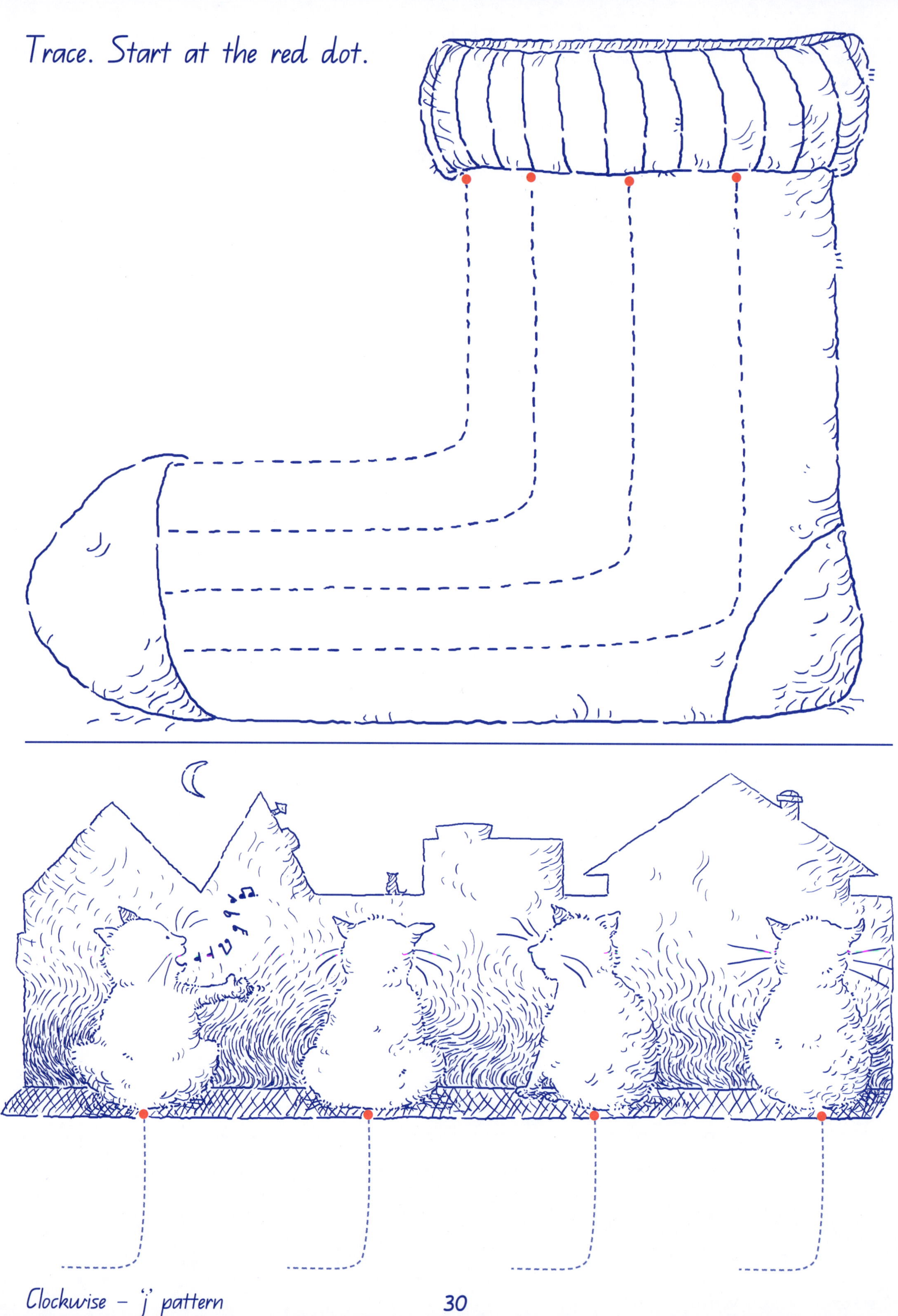

Trace. Start at the red dot.

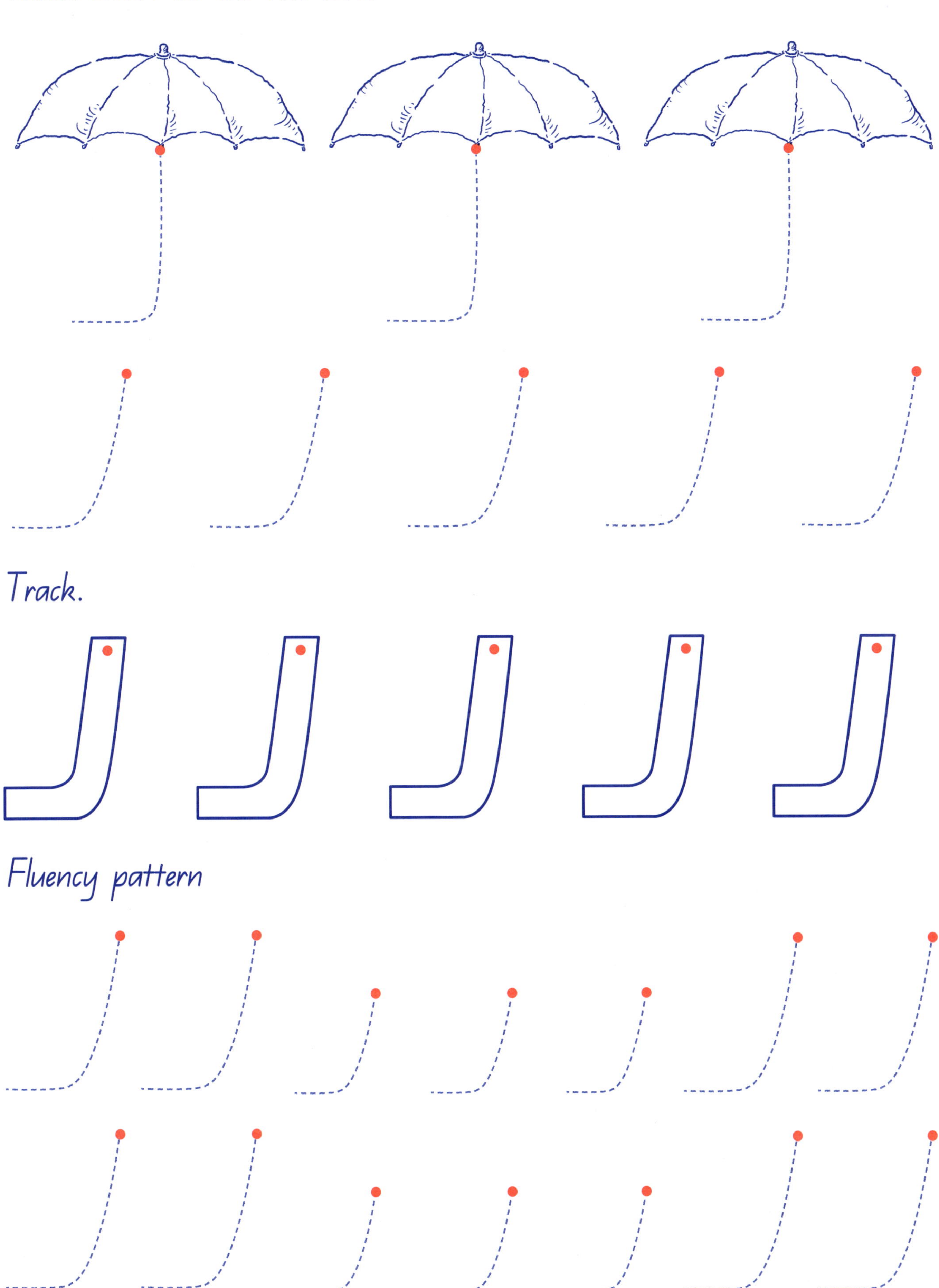

Track.

Fluency pattern

Track. Start at the red dot.

Track. Start at the red dot.

Trace.

Fluency pattern

Track. Start at the red dot.

Trace.

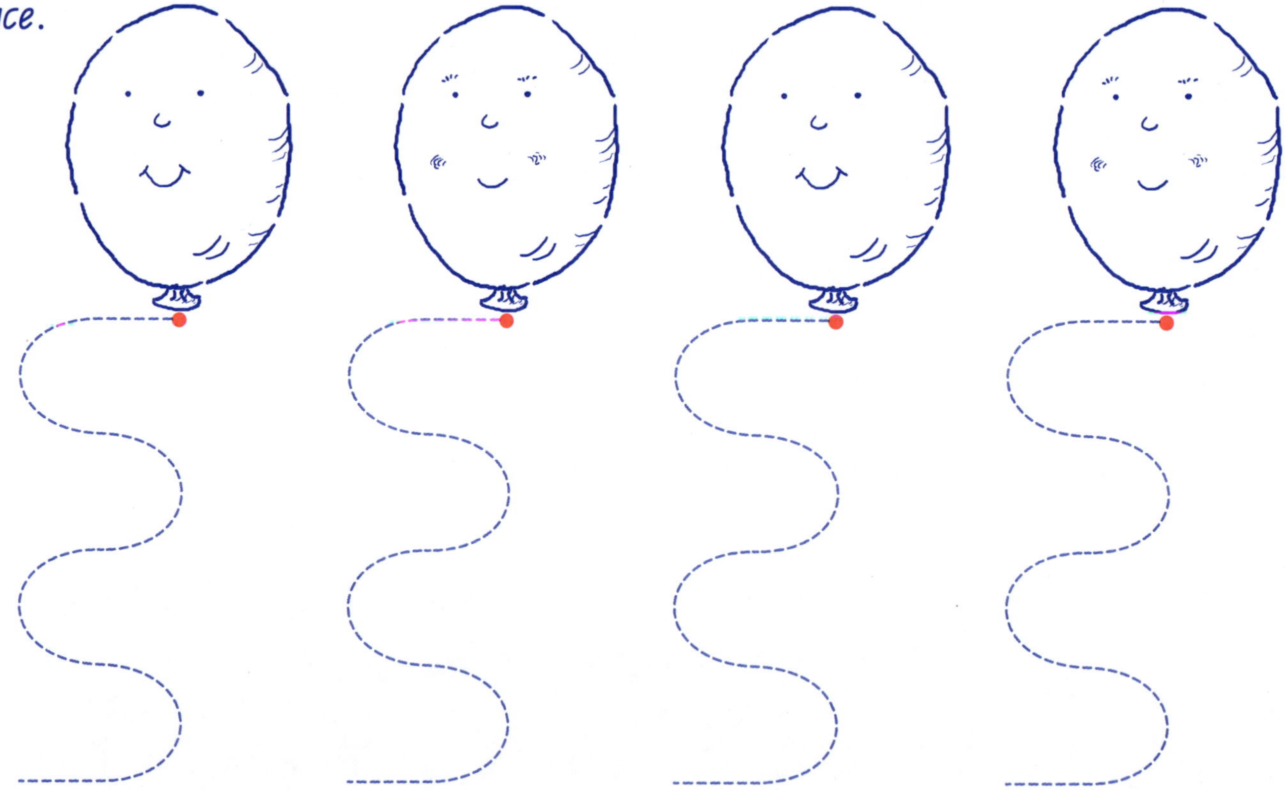

Trace. Start at the red dot.

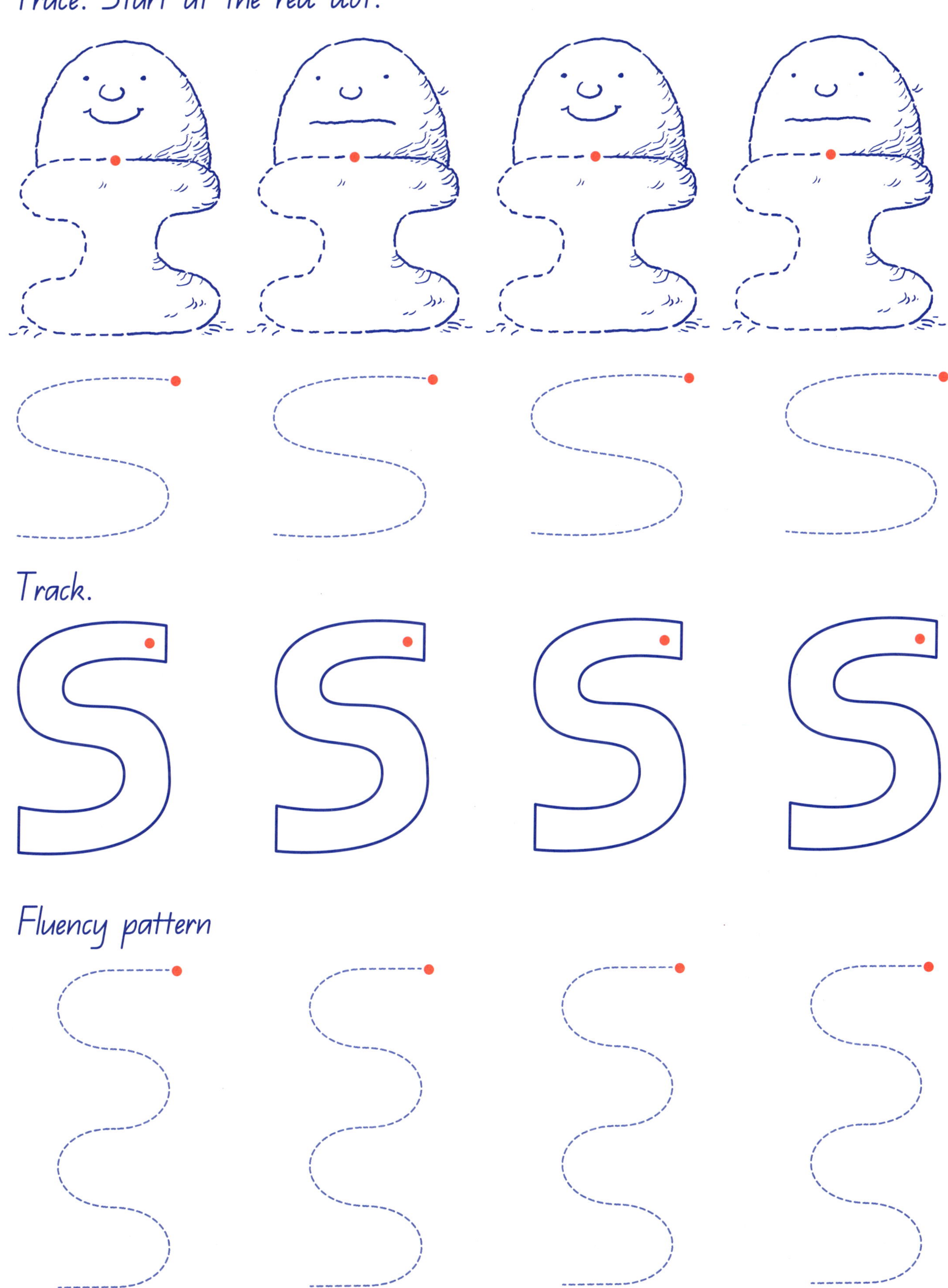

Track.

Fluency pattern

Trace and track. Start at the red dot.

Trace and track. Start at the red dot.

Trace and track. Start at the red dot.

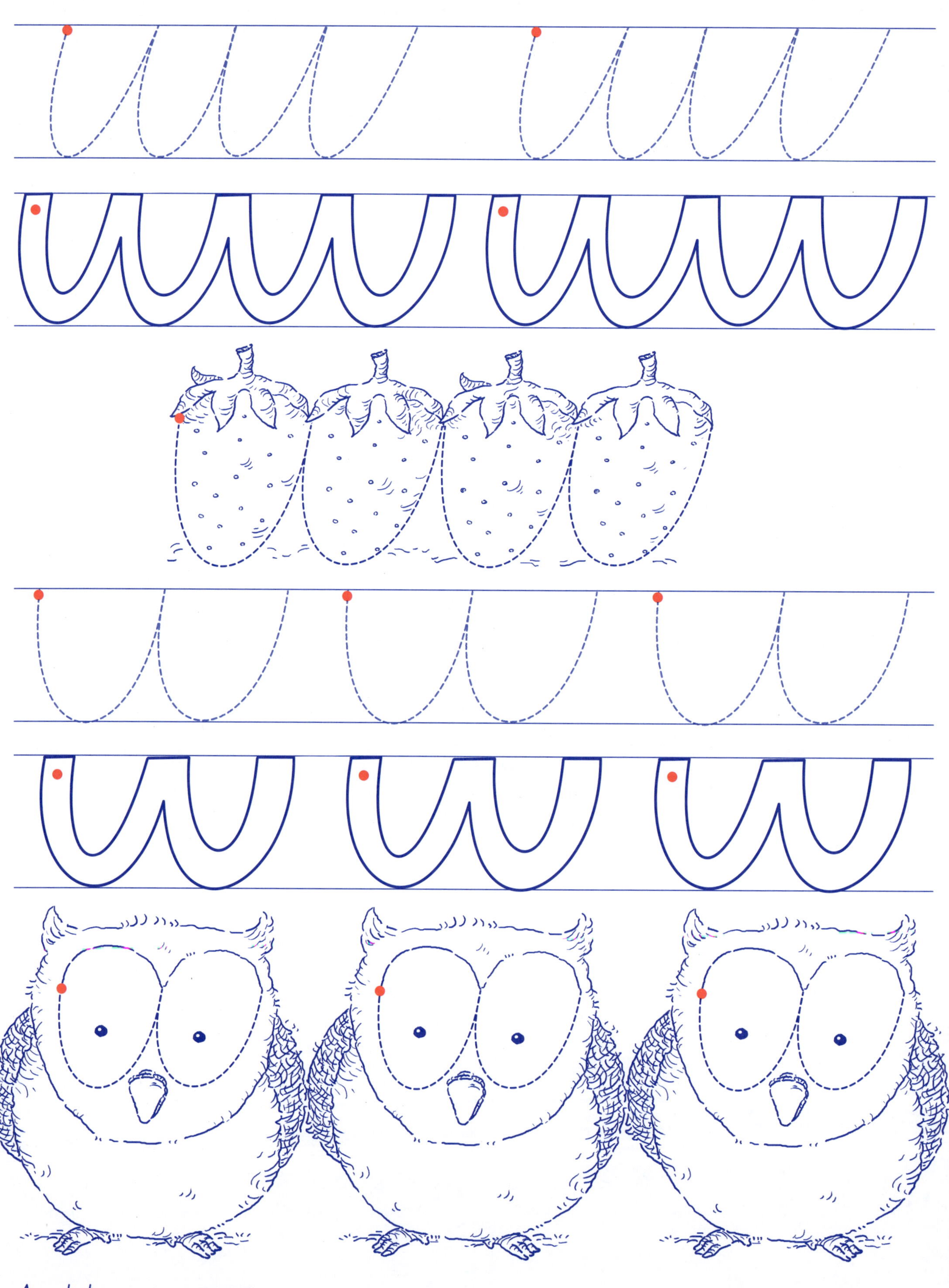

Trace and track. Start at the red dot.

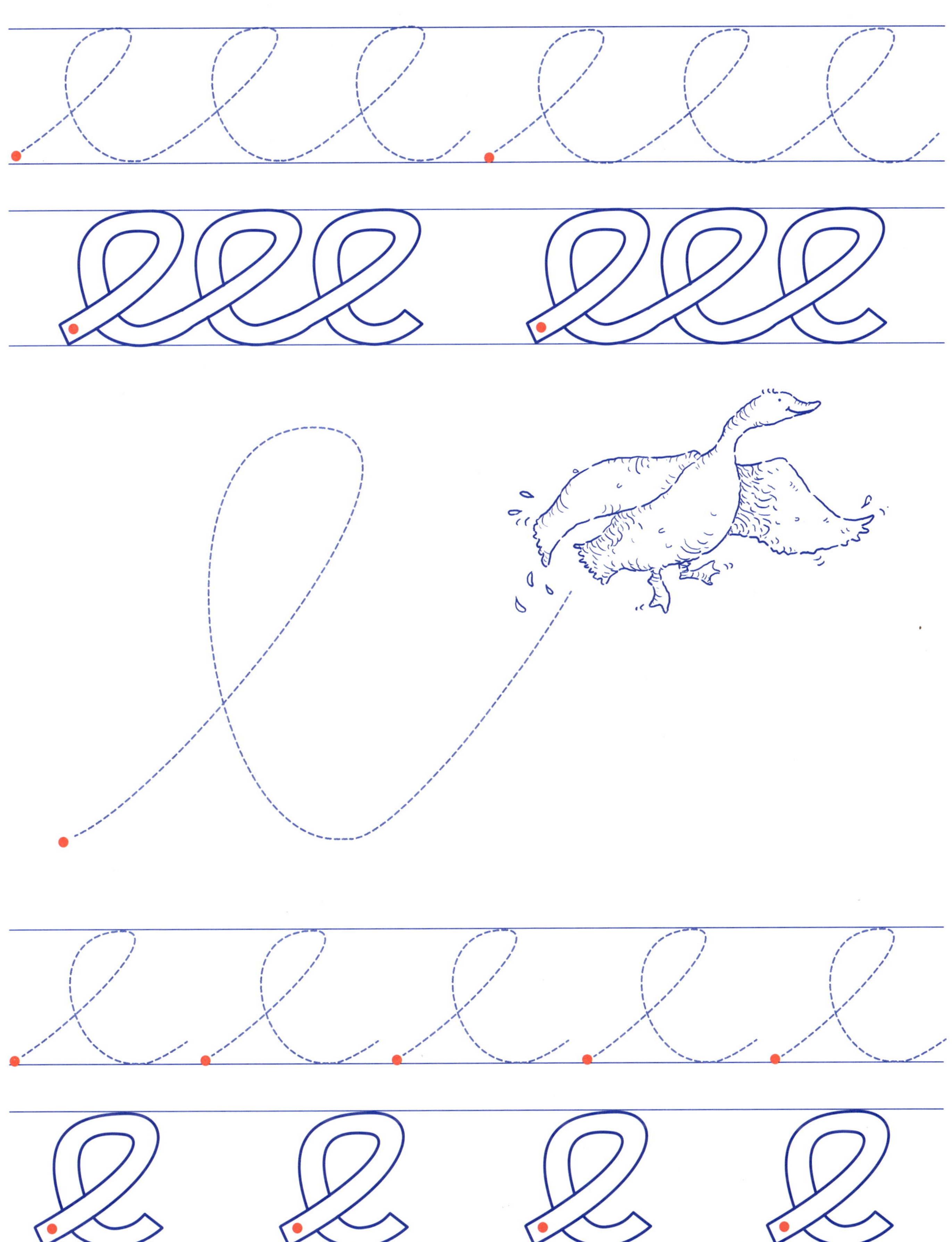

Trace and track. Start at the red dot.

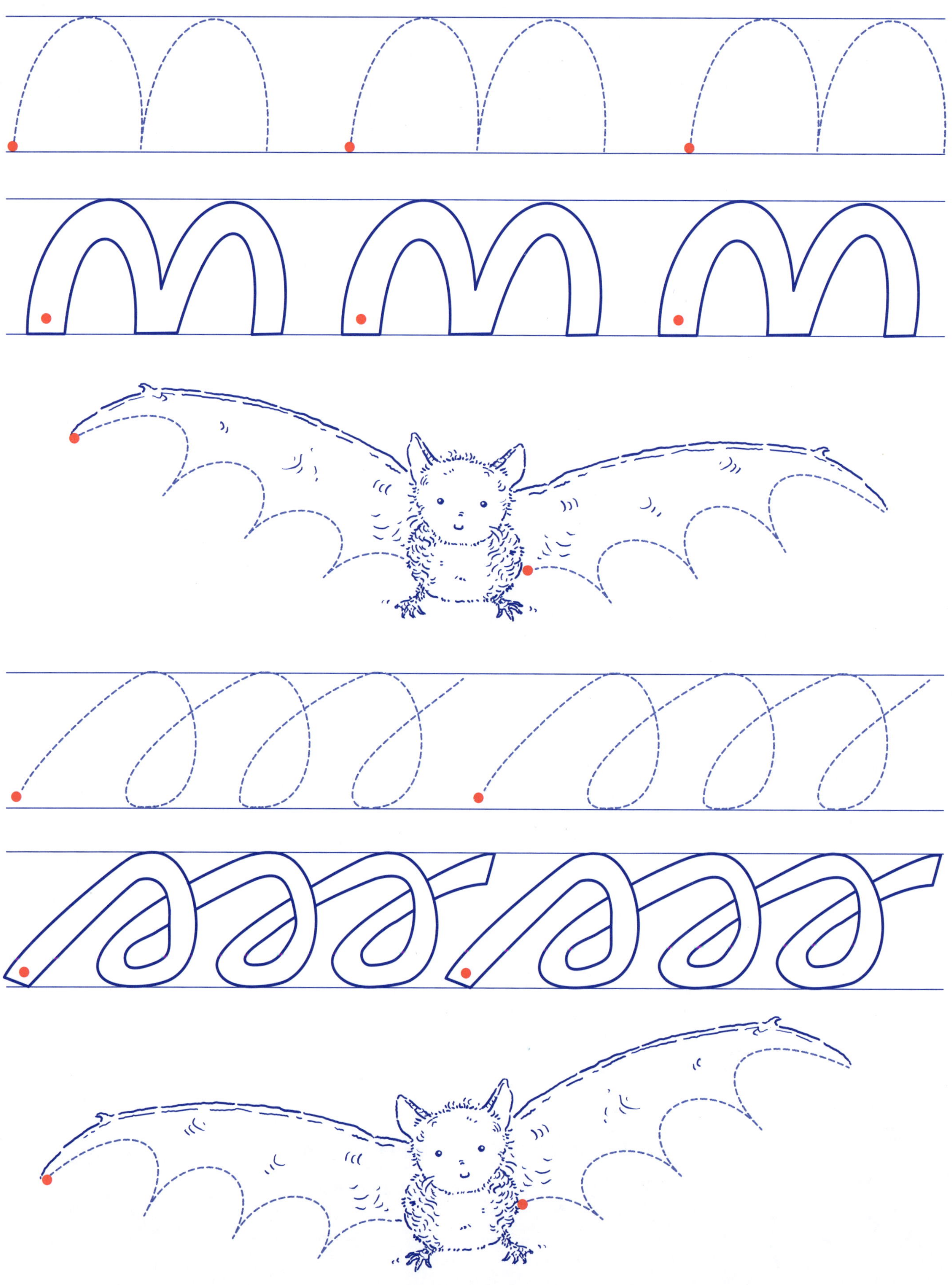

Trace and track. Start at the red dot.

Trace and track. Start at the red dot.

Trace and track. Start at the red dot.

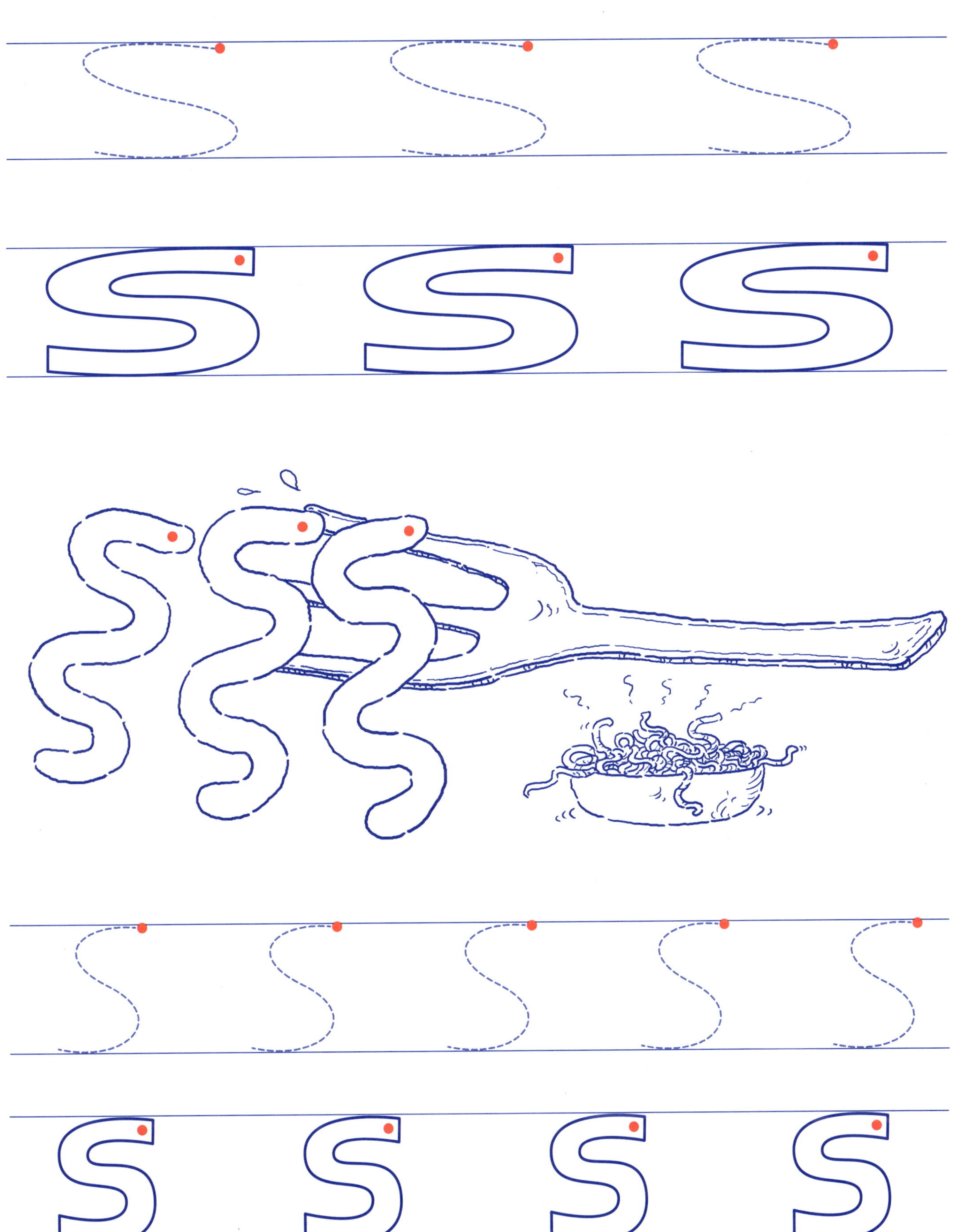

Trace.

Trace.

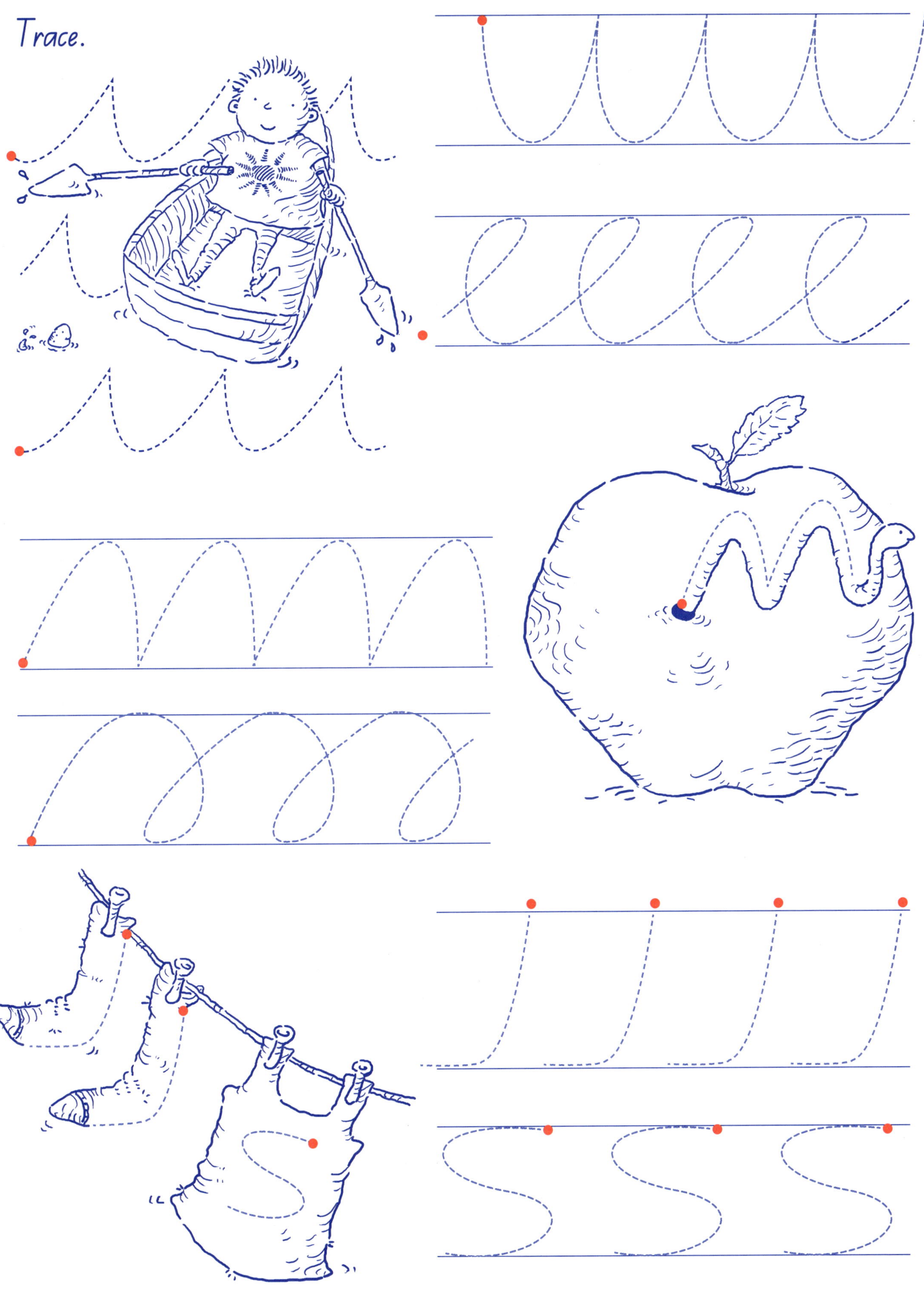

Trace.

Trace.

Congratulations ________________________.

Your writing is wonderful.

____

Teacher

____

Date

Well done ________________________.

Your writing is improving.

____

Teacher

____

Date